Searchers:

A Quick Guide to Researching, Evaluating, and Documenting Electronic Sources

2007 Edition

Carol Lea Clark

University of Texas at El Paso

FOUNTAINHEAD PRESS

Book design by Donovan & Gilhooley
Cover design by Stone House Art, Linda Beaupré

Copyright 2008 by Fountainhead Press

All rights reserved. No part of this book may be reproduced or utilized in any form or by any means, electronic or mechanical, including photocopying and recording, or by any information storage and retrieval system, without written permission from the publisher.

Books may be purchased for educational purposes.

For information, please call or write:

>1-800-586-0330

>Fountainhead Press
>100 W. Southlake Blvd. Suite 142, #350
>Southlake, TX 76092

Web site: www.fountainheadpress.com
Email: customerservice@fountainheadpress.com

Third Edition

ISBN 1-59871-006-9

Printed in the United States of America

Thanks to Amber Lea Clark for her assistance in research for this book.

Table of Contents

Chapter 1: Getting Started **1**
    Research Sources Professors Expect 2
    Make a Research Plan 4
    Understanding and Evaluating Sources 6
    Primary Sources 6
    Types of Primary Sources 7
    Secondary Sources 8
    Types of Secondary Sources 8
    Tertiary Sources 8
    Types of Tertiary Sources 8
    Evaluate Web Sources 9
    Use Computer Technology to Enhance Research and Writing 11
    Create Links to Your Sources with Bookmarks (Favorites) 11
    "Cut and Paste" Text to Facilitate Note Taking 12
    Use Microsoft Word's Comment Feature to Label Quotes 14
    Use Email to Transmit Paper Drafts 15
    Locate Assignments and Join Discussions on Your Class Web Site ... 17

Chapter 2: Library Tools **19**
    Library Computerized Catalogs 19
    Types of Searches 20
    Library Databases 21
    Frequently Listed Databases 22
    Government Documents 24

Chapter 3: Web Search Engines and Directories 25
    Equal but Different: Try These Search Engines 26
    Other Search Engines to Try 31
    Librarian-Reviewed Directories and Search Engines. 33
    Government Documents 36

Chapter 4: The Invisible Web 39
    Online Databases. 39
    Magazines and Newspapers 41
    Examples of Popular Newspapers and Magazines 42
    Web Links to Newspapers and Magazines 44

Chapter 5: Documentation. 45
    Avoid Plagiarism 45
    Documenting Sources 46
    Challenges in Documenting Electronic Publications 47
    Finding the Persistent Link 47
    Finding Page Numbers. 48
    MLA Style 48
    Bibliographical Documentation 48
    MLA Parenthetical or (In-text) Documentation 51
    APA Style. 53
    Bibliographical Documentation 53
    APA Parenthetical or (In-text) Documentation 56

CHAPTER ONE:
Getting Started

In the United States, we benefit from the centuries-old tradition of free access to information. Traditionally, libraries have been places where individuals could locate data and texts on almost any topic. Indeed, the concept "library" means collections of texts and other materials. Because of open libraries, one did not have to be rich or powerful to have access to information. People of modest means could examine books and other materials they could not afford to purchase. Today, the development of computers and the Internet have vastly extended the idea of free access to information.

What knowledge defines a well-educated person is changing because of the information revolution. The trend is away from memorization and toward what is called "information literacy" which means that one possesses set skills needed to find, retrieve, analyze, and use information.

In some ways, today is a great time to be a college student researcher. Information from around the world is available with a few clicks of a computer mouse. The list of resources is virtually endless: email, computerized card catalogs, library databases, Web sites, and so on. Entire companies exist to develop easier ways to find information. But therein lies the problem—what appears to be the entire knowledge base of human history is available through a computer connected to the Internet. Some have called this information overload "data smog" because the immensity of data can actually obscure the needed information. When faced with the endless information available from books, periodicals, the Internet, television, etc., it may be helpful to remember three things:

- Research on the Internet is more complicated than just entering a few key words in a search engine. Knowing a few techniques described in this book can greatly increase your chances of finding good information through search engines and directories.

- You cannot find everything on the Internet through search engines and directories. An immense "invisible Web" of information, including subject-specific databases and periodicals, must be accessed through gateway Web pages.

- Not everything is on the Internet. Copyright protection prevents much current information published in books or periodicals from being posted on the Internet. Using your college library is essential in a quality research process—both the computerized card catalog and the computerized databases.

Research Sources Professors Expect

You have been assigned a research paper or project. What does your professor expect of you? First of all, that you understand the assignment: What specifically does your professor want you to research? Do you have instructions about what kinds of sources your professor wants? Are restrictions put on what Internet or database sources you can use? Possibly, your instructor has specified that you need to use books, journals, major magazines and newspapers, and certain Web-based information. This means that you are to use reputable sources to obtain a balanced, impartial viewpoint about your topic. So, how do you find these sources?

- **Books:** College libraries collect scholarly books that are carefully researched and reviewed by authorities in the book's field. Look for recently published books rather than older books, even if they are on your topic. Locate scholarly books through the computerized catalog at your college (See Chapter 2).

- **Scholarly journals:** Your instructor means peer-reviewed journals in which the authors have documented their sources. Your library should have print indexes to journals in which you can look up your topic. You may also be able to find journal articles—sometimes in full text—through the online databases offered by your college library (See Chapter 2). For example, try JSTOR: Electronic Journal Archive which offers full-text versions of more than 300 journals in a variety of fields or Academic Search Premier, which indexes more than 4,000 journals, magazines, and newspapers.

- **Major magazines and newspapers:** You can locate full-text articles directly from the online versions of major print magazines and newspapers (See Chapter 4). Often, these publications charge a fee for articles not published recently. However, you can often find the same articles free through library databases (See Chapter 2).

- **Web-based information:** The problem with Web-based information is that anyone with some knowledge of computers can put up a Web site on the Internet. Thus, information from Web sites must be carefully evaluated as to author, publishing organization, etc. (see section in this chapter on How to Evaluate Web Sources). One way to deal with this problem is to find Web information through the librarian-generated indexes and search engines which screen Web sites for credibility (See Chapter 3). Another is to access databases maintained by credible organizations such as the National Institutes of Health, Bureau of the Census, etc. (See Chapter 4).

As you use the methods above to find sources for your paper or project, realize that your topic influences your choice of reference materials. If you are writing about a literary topic such as Shakespeare's *Othello*, you will find a number of relevant books and journal articles. If your topic is more contemporary, such as the current status of the Space Shuttle flights, you may be able to find some books or journal articles for background information, but you will need to use recent magazine and newspaper articles to find the latest information.

As you examine your sources, remember that gathering the information should help you discover what you think about your topic, not just what others think. This will enable you to create a paper based on your ideas and opinions, with source materials supporting your position.

Make a Research Plan

Will you be using the Internet simply as one research tool along with print texts? For many topics, some of the most current information can be found electronically, and it can greatly enhance your information collection. Will you be gathering all your information from the Internet? Not all topics have equal coverage on the Internet, but for many subjects (if your instructor agrees), you can collect everything you need without leaving your computer terminal.

When making a research plan, you need to consider your assignment. Does it say, "Write an argumentative essay about an environmental problem such as toxic waste or acid rain?" If so, you know you need to narrow the topic from the environment in general to a more specific topic such as toxic waste. Perhaps narrow it to an even more specific topic such as programs for nuclear waste disposal or the recycling of environmentally damaging substances. If you aren't sure what specific topic interests you, you will need to look first at some general sources about the environment to help you choose a topic. Several research resources on the Web can help you narrow a topic and then gather information about it.

For example, connect to Hot Paper Topics at http://library.sau.edu/bestinfo/Hot/hotindex.htm, and find links to references collected by librarians at the O'Keefe Library on popular paper topics such as affirmative action and school vouchers. Browse through the subject links, and you may find a topic that interests you. Then you can do additional research on the topic using other types of electronic resources discussed in this book. See also other librarian-reviewed indexes and search engines in Chapter 2, which also can be used for topic exploration.

O'Keefe Library
St. Ambrose University

Best Information on the Net

SAUOME

Resources by Major
Hot Paper Topics
Alphabetical Index

Student Resources
Faculty Resources
Online Reference Resources
Disability Resources
Current Events
Resources for Librarians
Library Home

Hot Paper Topics

Affirmative Action

Article Files and Indexes to Hot Topics

Attack on America / Terrorism

Bioethical Issues

Censorship

Death Penalty

Drug Issues

Enron

Gender Issues

Gun Control

Health Care Reform

Help for Term Paper Writers

Human Rights

Identity Theft

Internet Issues

Media Issues

Miscellaneous Issues

Nanotechnology

Plagiarism

Hot Paper Topics, http://library.sau.edu/bestinfo/Hot/hotindex.htm, collects librarian-screened Web sites on topics popular with college students.

Once you have decided on a narrow topic, you can use other subject indexes, keyword search engines, full-text databases, and media links to find additional resources. As you locate resources, assemble them in a working bibliography, which will help you keep track of them as potential resources. Remember that research is a recursive process. As you explore sources, you may find yourself changing the narrow topic you have selected, and this will require you to find additional sources. Even when you reach the writing stage of your project, you still may need to locate information sources to fill holes in your argument. The research is not complete until the project is complete.

Understanding and Evaluating Sources

When conducting research, students must understand the significance of the types of sources they use as evidence. Certain sources are more valued than others and offer a higher degree of support to claims. Most sources are categorized as either primary or secondary. Both primary and secondary sources are further categorized into an unofficial hierarchy of best or most valued sources. This determination is based upon several qualifying factors such as originality, credibility; wealth of scope of research involved, ethos of the author, etc. Therefore, it is imperative that students choose a variety of highly credible sources to produce their own work of research and writing. The following definitions and examples below provide a framework for understanding sources acceptable in academic research and writing. Both print and electronic sources can be of three types: primary, secondary, and tertiary. To strengthen the research component of your project, use at least some primary sources in your writing, if they are available. For example, if you are writing a critique of the president's State of the Union speech, find a copy of the original speech, perhaps at the White House site, http://www.whitehouse.gov, or at the online New York Times, http://www.nytimes.com, which often offers full text of speeches. Then locate commentaries on his speeches, which would be secondary sources.

Primary Sources

Primary sources are those records generated by a particular event or time period, by those who participated in or witnessed it such as a records containing information documented at or about the time of the event, as opposed to compiled or secondary information; primary sources are generally more reliable than secondary sources. Primary sources contain original information and are usually the place where the original information first appears. A primary source is a person, place, or thing that provides firsthand

GETTING STARTED   7

> ### Research Strategies for Finding Electronic Sources
>
> 1. Using a subject index, either in a search engine such as Yahoo! (page 27) or a librarians' subject index (page 20), browse sites in your general topic. See what kinds of information are available on what specific topics.
> 2. Check online media links for articles on your general topics (page 44).
> 3. Search one or more of your library's full-text periodical databases for your general topic and, through them, obtain journal and magazine articles (page 19).
> 4. Narrow your search to a topic specific enough to write about in the length of research paper you are assigned.
> 5. Use one or more keyword search engines to locate additional relevant sites (page 21). Repeat steps one to three for your specific topic.
> 6. Compile the resources you have identified into a working bibliography.

information about something. Primary sources can be defined in two ways. (1) A document or other sort of evidence written or created during the time under study. Primary sources offer an inside view of a particular event. (2) In science, an original report of research that has not been condensed or interpreted. Because of the Internet, it is now easier for students to find primary sources such as speeches or research reports.

Types of Primary Sources

Examples of primary sources include autobiographies, speeches, official records, news film footage, original manuscripts, records, or documents providing original research or documentation, photographs, drawings, letters, diaries, books, minutes of meetings, films, posters, play scripts, speeches, songs, a first person account, interviews, speeches, results of experiments or original research, literary works, autobiographies, original theories, oral histories, a lab report, a painting, an original musical score or a court transcript, court reports, artifacts or physical objects, field research reports, technical reports, research journal articles, and conference proceedings.

Secondary Sources

A secondary source is any source that is not first hand. Secondary sources are those records generated by an event but written by non-participants of the event. Secondary sources are based on or derived from primary sources but have been interpreted or analyzed. Secondary sources are one step removed from the event being described but provide the background necessary to understand the primary sources. Secondary sources usually describe, summarize, analyze, evaluate, derive from, or are based on primary source material. Secondary sources are texts based on primary sources, and involve generalization, analysis, synthesis, interpretation, or evaluation. Information written by an authority who reports on an event, person, place or thing; i.e., a biography, is a secondary source; an autobiography is a primary source. A secondary source contains information that other people have gathered and interpreted, extended, analyzed, or evaluated.

Types of Secondary Sources

Examples of secondary sources are those that include magazine and journal articles, literary criticism, biographies, and encyclopedia articles which analyze or interpret primary sources. Others are textbooks, journal articles, histories, criticisms, commentaries, encyclopedias, and other materials that are not original manuscripts. Sometimes you can locate original sources by examining the works cited of a secondary source.

Tertiary Sources

A tertiary source is a selection and compilation of primary and secondary sources.

Types of Tertiary Sources

Examples of tertiary sources include almanacs, dictionaries, encyclopedias, and fact books, reference material that synthesizes work already reported in primary or secondary sources.

Evaluate Web Sources

Many people tend to believe what they see in print. They may think that if information is in a book or a news magazine, it must be true. If you read critically, however, you know that all sources must be evaluated. Does a source give a balanced reporting of the evidence, or does it display bias? What resource sources are cited? What authorities are utilized? With the Internet, perhaps even more than with print texts, it is important to evaluate your sources. Undoubtedly, much reliable and valuable information is published through the Web, and you should not hesitate to use sources that, in your judgment, are credible. Remember, though, not all information on the Web is accurate. Anyone with a Web connection and a little knowledge can create a site, and automated search engines will include that site in their databases. Also, many sites are commercial and may have their own marketing reasons for promoting certain information. Before relying on information, ask yourself the following questions listed in "How to Evaluate Web Sources."

You may intentionally study biased sources on the Web if the material are primary texts such as home pages of political candidates, special interest groups, or companies selling products. If so, do not take their information at face value. Indeed, you can make your evaluation of biased texts part of your argument. You could, for example, compare what a company selling a health food supplement such as ginkgo biloba or omega 3 oils says about that product with what you read in your search of other texts related to that product (including scientific studies). One of the Web's revolutionary aspects is that individuals and organizations can put their side of the story directly before the public. It is part of your job as a Web consumer to evaluate critically the motivation or validity of these direct-to-the-public texts.

How to Evaluate Web Sources

Who Is the Author?

An important first step in establishing credibility of a Web site is considering the authorship. Credible authors that publish on the Internet generally will give a brief statement of their qualifications, or they may post a resume.- If your article was published in a magazine or newspaper, search the publication for other articles by the same author. If the author has an affiliation with a university, you can search the university's Web site for additional information about the author.- You can also do a keyword search for that person through a search engine.

Who Is the Publisher?

The publisher often is as important as the author.- If the text was published in a reputable journal, magazine, or newspaper, the credibility of the publication attaches to the article. If your text was published on a Web site, not a publication's Web site, you need to employ other methods to assess the credibility of the publisher.

If you found the Web site through one of the librarian-research engines (pages 33-36), for example, you know the site has been evaluated and found acceptable for academic use.

You may be able to tell if the Web site is linked to an organization by looking at the URL or Web address. The organization or company name in the URL, such as http://www.exxon.com indicates that the material is published on the Exxon Web site. The suffix of the URL is also helpful: .edu means an educational or research institution, .gov for government resources, .com or .net for commercial products or commercially-sponsored sites.

Does the Document Appear Professional?

Credible sources go through an editing and reviewing process. Does the text look balanced and fair? Watch for grammatical errors, punctuation errors, misspellings, and other errors that would have been caught during an editing process. Ask yourself whether the graphics of the site add to or detract from the authoritativeness of the site.

Continued on next page

How to Evaluate Web Sources (Continued)

Does It Provide Information about Sources?

Look for a list of references at the end of the document and/or informal references-to sources in the text. Where did the author get his or her information? If you cannot tell where the information came from, why should you trust it? It is a good idea to choose a few of the references the author mentions and validate them by making sure that the books or journal articles used actually exist and are represented fairly.

Is It Current?

Look for a publication date or a "last updated" date. Most credible sources will have a date.- Currency can also be checked by testing out the links on the page.- Are the links still up-to-date and useable?- Do the graphics or photos display?

What Is the Purpose?

Was the Web site created to offer trustworthy information, to persuade, to sell, or for some other reason? If the site is selling anything, use its content only with great caution.

Use Computer Technology to Enhance Research and Writing

Today's Web-browsing and word-processing programs offer a number of features that can make your research collection, organization, and revising much easier than recording information by handwriting.

Create Links to Your Sources with Bookmarks (Favorites)

Internet Explorer and other Web-browsing programs have a built-in feature to create bookmarks for pages you would like to return to in the future, and you can use this feature to create a folder of links for a particular research project. In Internet Explorer, bookmarks are called *Favorites*. Add a source to your list of *Favorites* by following these steps:

1. Direct your browser to the page that you want to add to your list.

2. Using the *Favorites* menu, click *Add to Favorites*.

3. When prompted, name the source.

4. Continue this process with other Web sources.

5. To open the link to a favorite source, use the *Favorites* menu, and click the page you want to open.

6. You can organize your list of sources by moving the links into subfolders. Using the *Favorites* menu, click on *Organize Favorites*.

7. When prompted, click *Create Folder*, type a name for the folder (perhaps the research topic), and then press *ENTER*.

8. Drag the links for sources in the list to the appropriate folders. Instead of dragging, you can also use the *Move to Folder* button instead.

"Cut and Paste" Text to Facilitate Note Taking

Like many other writers, you can use "cut and paste" computer technology to make note taking easy. For example, say you want to copy a section of a *Salon* article about recycling from the magazine's Web site:

1. Open a new document in Microsoft Word.

2. Display the text of your source in Internet Explorer.

3. Highlight a section of the text you want to save and use the *Edit* menu in Microsoft Word to copy the text. See the image on the next page that shows part of the article highlighted.

4. Paste the text into your Microsoft Word screen and put quote marks around the quoted text. Similar to the image below, add bibliographic information about the source to the top of the Word file and your own remarks about the quote.

RECYCLING IS GREAT -- UNLESS YOU LIVE CLOSE TO WHERE IT'S HAPPENING.

BY DAVID BACON | HUNTINGTON PARK, CALIF. --
recycling has an environmentally friendly image. Reusing the basic materials of everyday life to ensure a sustainable future for the planet has almost becomes God's work. It has also become big business, especially in places of enormous consumption and waste like Los Angeles.

Some 20 years ago, when L.A. drew up its master plan, the recycling industry hardly existed. Today industrial facilities that process glass, metal and concrete are mushrooming. But some people living in Los Angeles have a hard time seeing recycling's green image. Their problem? They live near the plants.

"There's always glass in the air here," complains Mercedes Arambula, whose home in the southeastern part of the metropolis is catty-corner from a huge Container Recycling facility. Mounds of broken glass rise to twice the height of an adult in the yard. Skip loaders constantly fill open truck trailers with it.

"I've lived here 18 years," she says. "My kids have asthma now, and my littlest one, who's 1 1/2, is always sick. I won't even let them play in the yard anymore. The trees around my house have all died anyway."

A neighbor, Ana Cano, wipes her finger across the dusty windshield of a parked van in front of her house. It sparkles and feels grainy. "Little by little, we're breathing this in," she says. "I feel like my

It is easy to copy quotes from electronic articles by using "cut and paste" technology. Highlight the material to be quoted and select Copy from the Edit menu in Microsoft Word.

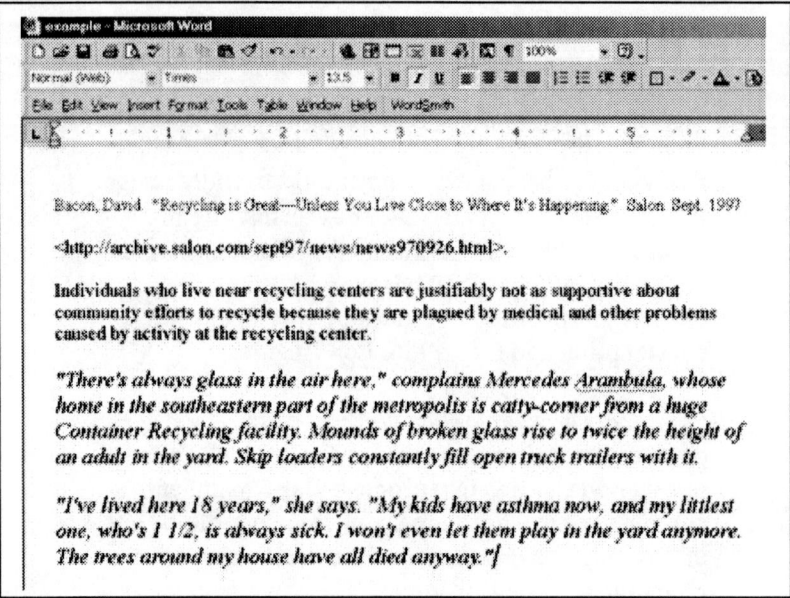

Paste the quote in an open Word document. Add bibliographic information and your comment about the quote.

You can continue to cut and paste sections of the article into the document and intersperse them with your own comments. Like the example in the image above, you may want to put quoted material in italics to distinguish it clearly from your own words. Later, you can convert quotes into summaries or paraphrases, if you wish.

Use Microsoft Word's Comment Feature to Label Quotes

One problem students often experience, when working with material from sources, is that source material is pasted as quotes into a draft, and information about the source can become lost or confused. If you use Microsoft's *Comment* feature to label each section associated with a particular source, that information is transferred when the wording is pasted into a new document. For example, if you were working on your notes about the *Salon* article (shown in the previous image), you can easily add bibliographic information about the source of the quote:

1. Highlight the portion of the text to be associated with the comment.

2. Go to the *Insert* menu and select *Comment*. In the box that appears below, type or cut and paste bibliographical information to be associated with that particular text. When you move the highlighted text to another document or a different location in a document, the comment will still be present and give bibliographical information. You can also use the *Comment* feature to ask yourself questions or leave suggestions for future revision. Windows XP utilizes the *View* menu and *Markup* feature to display *Comments*.

Use Email to Transmit Paper Drafts

Have you ever lost a draft of a paper or other assignment because the disk you used to save your document became corrupted, and your document would not open? Of course, you can have two disks and record each draft of your paper on both disks which would reduce the risk of losing a paper draft. Another popular way to prevent the loss of your work is to email each draft to yourself as an email attachment. This second method has two advantages: If you are working on your paper both at home and at a computer on campus, you can transport the paper back and forth by email, eliminating the disk problem. Also, if you do not erase the emails containing your drafts as attachments, you have a record of each draft in case you want to retrieve text from an earlier draft.

Most email programs, such as Yahoo! Mail, allow you to easily attach a text file as an attachment. Simply display the compose message screen, usually by clicking on *New Message* or *Compose Message*, and fill in the *To:* box with your own email address. Then click on *Attachments* and follow the program's instructions for attaching a file. Send the email, and it will appear in your email message inbox.

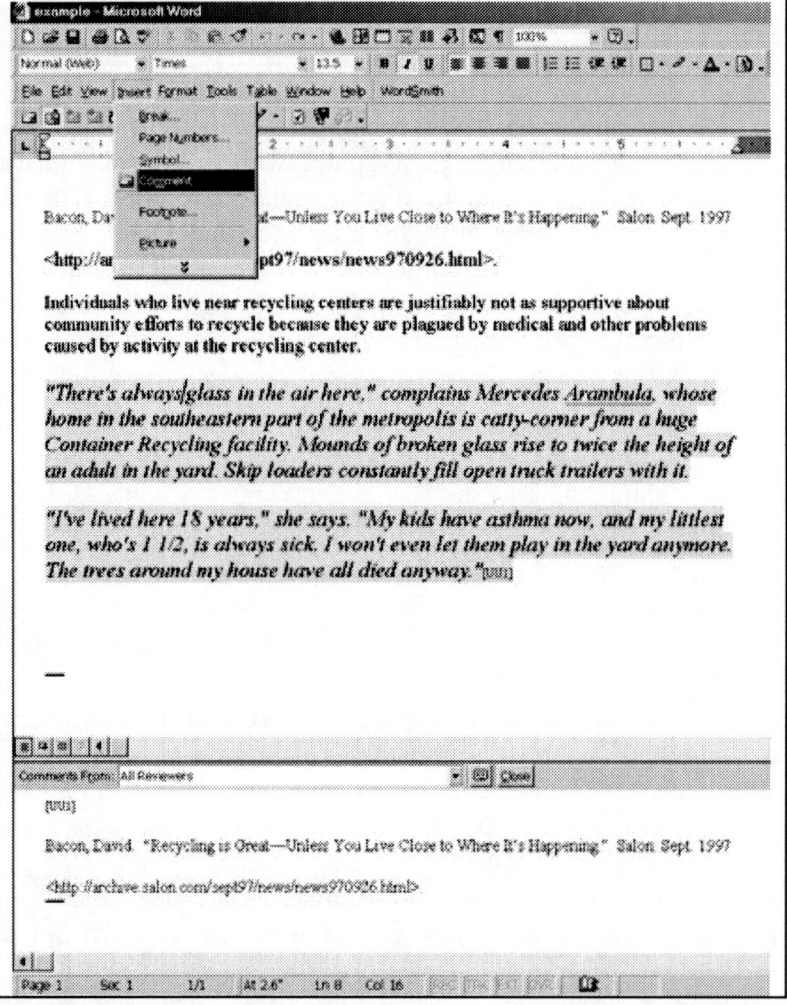

Use Microsoft Word's Comment feature to record bibliographic information about the source of a quote. Then, when you copy and paste the quote into your draft, the source information transfers to your draft document.

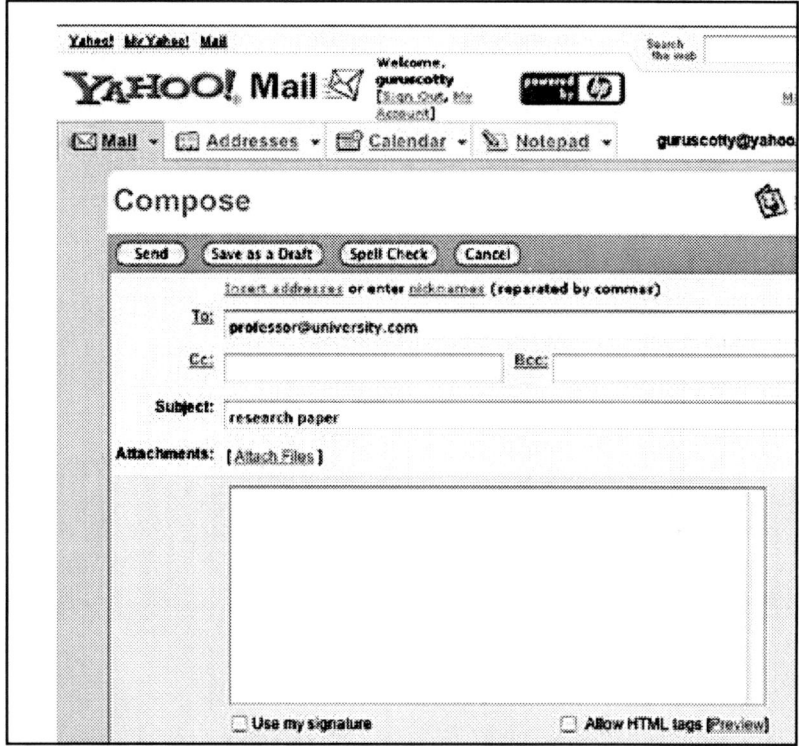

Yahoo! and other email programs allow you to attach files easily, such as paper drafts, and email them to yourself.

Locate Assignments and Join Discussions on Your Class Web Site

More and more professors are making use of Web-based technology to deliver all or part of a college course. On the simplest level, a professor may post a syllabus containing course policies and due dates on a Web page. At the most complex, a class is actually held in cyberspace, either in hybrid part-classroom/part-online format or completely online.

In many cases, the online course components may require a login and password to access materials. This policy restricts the use of the text, images, sound, and other types of files to the instructor and the students, thus protecting the professor's work and also allowing certain third-party copyrighted works to be included under the copyright "fair use" policy.

WebCT is a popular course-management software used to deliver course content such as syllabi and assignments, as well as allowing online class chat, email, and discussions.

Your instructor may make use of course management software (CMS) such as WebCT or Blackboard to deliver the course content. The software allows instructors easily to post syllabi, assignments, and other files. In addition, CMS includes interactive features such as real-time chat rooms, email, and discussion boards that allow you to communicate with classmates and the instructor.

CHAPTER 2:
Library Tools

Today's college libraries are still the best sources for current information published in books and periodicals. In addition to the familiar hard-cover books and print periodicals, libraries are increasingly offering digital resources. As a college student, you have entry through your library Web site to online books and periodical databases which have restricted access, resources you can not find directly on the Internet without paying fees.

Library Computerized Catalogs

A library computerized catalog provides bibliographical information about the library's collection. Likely, you can find call numbers and other essential location information about thousands of books, photos, videos, journals, and other items. Generally, catalogs can be accessed by keyword, subject, author, title, and call number. You may also find books which are available in digital form through the card catalog.

On the library home page, you will find links to other information and services such as database searches, interlibrary loan, and course reserves.

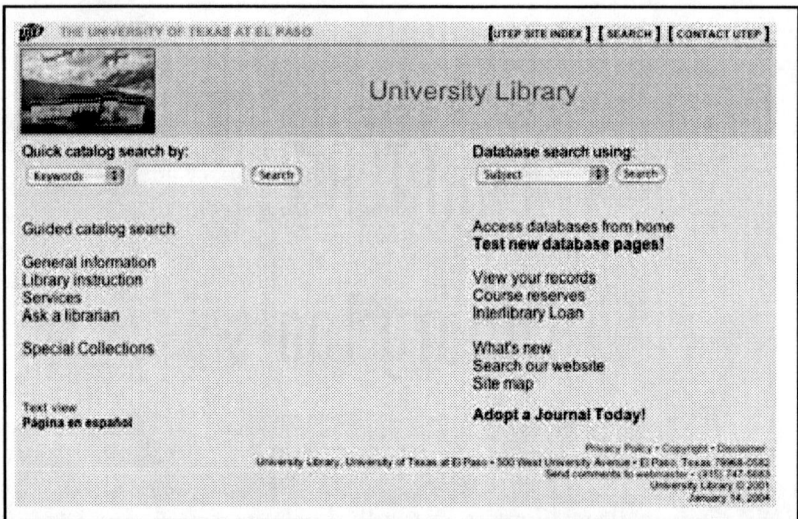

This university library Web site affords quick access to the computerized catalog, allowing searches by keywords, subject, author, title, and call number.

Types of Searches

- Keyword—Unless you know the author or title of a book, keyword is the best type of search because it finds the search word or words anywhere in the bibliographical citation.

    Example: water quality

- Title—Type the exact order of words in the title.

    Example: History of the United Kingdom

- Author—Type the author's name, putting the last name first. You don't need to include a comma.

    Example: Miller Henry J.

- Subject—Type the exact Library of Congress subject heading.

    Example: Spanish language – Grammar, Historical

- Call Number—Type the exact call number.

    Example: B851 .P49 2004

Library Databases

College and university libraries increasingly rely on databases to provide digital versions of articles published in journals, magazines, newspapers, as well as other publications and materials. Generally, the databases are available to students and faculty through the Internet via the library home page, though a library card and a password may be required for off-campus access.

Library databases make use of online forms similar to that of a library computerized catalog. Searches are by subject, title, author, and name of publication. Advanced search features are available. Some databases provide full text of articles published in newspapers, journals, and magazines. Others give publication information only, such as title, author, publication, date of publication, and an abstract of the article. Popular databases include Lexis-Nexis Academic Universe, Academic Search Premier, and JSTOR.

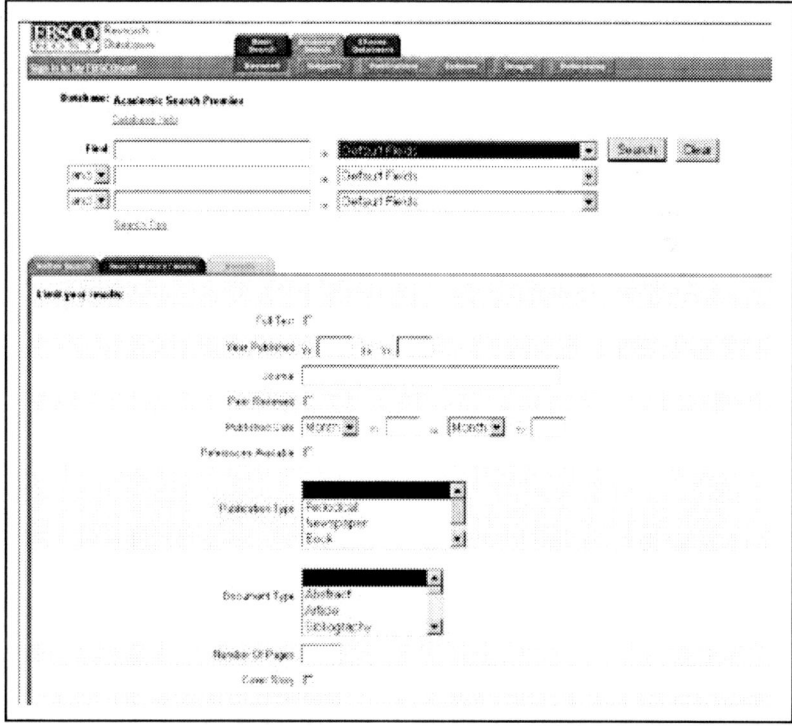

Academic Search Premier, one of the full-text databases provided by EBSCOhost, is available at many colleges and universities.

Frequently Listed Databases

Academic Search Complete
This is an EBSCOhost database that contains full-text from academic journals, books, magazines, and newspapers. Fields include arts, humanities, social sciences, general science, computer science, education and multicultural studies. It also offers abstracts of additional journals (coverage from 1965 to present).

ArticleFirst (FirstSearch)
This is a searchable index of articles taken from the contents of journals in science, technology, medicine, social science, business, humanities, and popular culture (full-text of selected articles from 1990-present).

InfoTrac Newspapers
This site provides access to full-text articles from international, national, and regional newspapers, including the *Austin American-Statesman, Dallas Morning News*, and *Houston Chronicle*.

INGENTA
Formerly known as Uncover, this database provides citations from 1988 to the present to articles from the tables of contents of journals and magazines that cover all disciplines. If the subscription of the university allows, you can purchase full-text articles. It can also be searched directly at http://www.ingentaconnect.com.

JSTOR: Electronic Journal Archive
This database contains full-text articles from multidisciplinary and discipline-specific collections, allowing libraries to customize their JSTOR archive to match their subject emphasized at their universities. Discipline-specific collections include business, ecology and botany, health sciences, language and literature, mathematics, and music.

LexisNexis Academic

This LexisNexis database features full-text coverage of topics such as legal, business, government, current news, and medicine. Sources include newspapers, broadcast transcripts, company financial information, and SEC filings.

Newspaper Source

An EBSCOHost database, Newspaper Source offers current news from around the world with updates from newspaper wire services, as well as national and international newspapers.

Project Muse

This database offers academic journal articles from the fields of literature, history, the arts, cultural studies, education, political science, gender studies, economics, area studies and others.

PsycInfo

This is an EBSCOhost bibliographic index that provides citations, abstracts, and some full text for the field of psychology taken from journal articles, book chapters, books, dissertations, and technical reports. The coverage includes the psychological aspects of related disciplines.

Readers' Guide Abstracts

This database corresponds to the printed *Readers' Guide to Periodical Literature*. It contains selected full-text articles from magazines on a wide variety of topics including news, arts, education, business, sports, health, consumer affairs, and others.

Worldcat

This is a FirstSearch database that provides access to library catalogs from around the world. The database contains bibliographic records describing books, journals, maps, musical scores, manuscripts, etc.

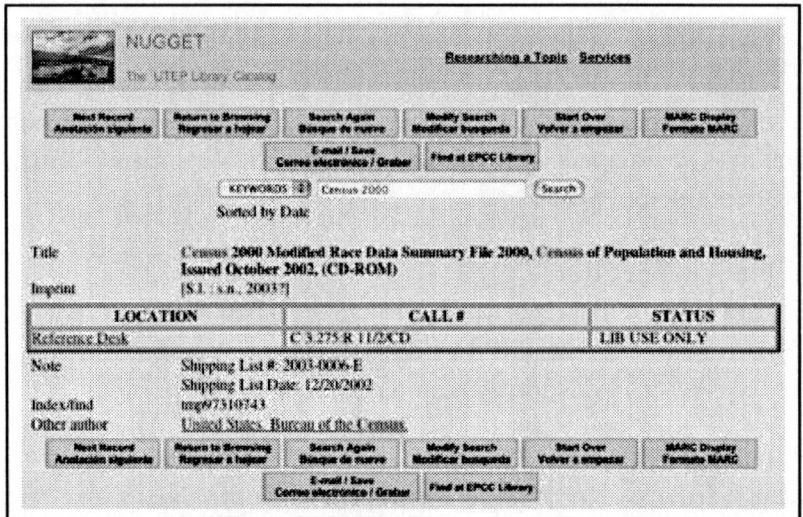

You can locate many government documents in your college library by doing a keyword search in your library's computerized catalog, if your library is a federal depository.

Government Documents

Government documents present a wealth of information for many contemporary events and issues. Your library may be a federal depository, which means that users can locate many federal documents onsite. If so, you can look up government sources in the online library catalog. The screen capture above shows the result of a keyword search in a university's online catalog for information about the 2000 United States Census.

Lexis-Nexis Congressional Universe
Congressional Universe offers an index to congressional publications, including pending legislation, the Federal Register, and other documents dating back to 1970.

Lexis-Nexis Government Periodicals Universe
Periodicals Universe gives access to periodicals published by U.S. government agencies from 1987 to the present.

CHAPTER 3:
Web Search Engines and Directories

The World Wide Web is an incredible resource for research. Through it, you can find full texts of pending legislation, searchable online editions of Shakespeare's plays, environmental impact statements, stock quotes, and much, much more. Finding the research sources you need, however, is not always easy. Research on the Web is far more than surfing. The Internet is immense, and its content is seemingly endless. For example, if you enter the word "environment" in one of the keyword search engines, you may receive thousands of "hits," or sites that relate to that topic from all over the world. How do you sift through all of that feedback in order to find information relevant to your topic? It is a problem that has not been completely solved on the Internet. However, some strategies will help.

Knowing how to use search engines to uncover data is an invaluable element of good research. There are many search engines available on the Web, but they are not all created equal. Keyword search engines allow the user to search their database of indexed Web sites for keywords such as "dog" or "plasma." They return a list of results or hits, each of which includes a description, the URL (Web address) and the name of the Web site.

Librarian-researched search engines and directories provide links to sources which have been pre-screened for academic use. A variety of Web sites offer government documents and other information about the federal government.

Equal but Different:
Try These Search Engines

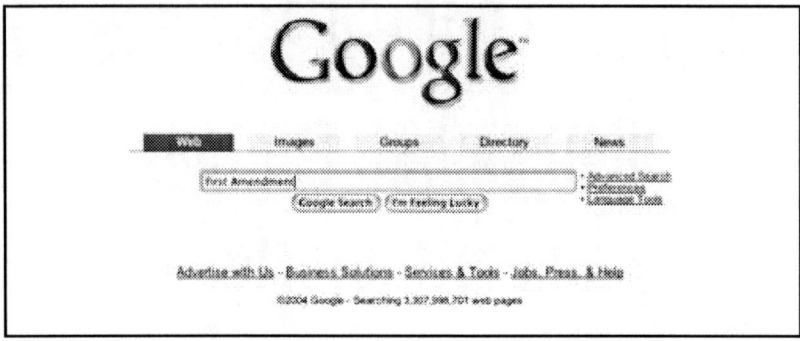

Google, the most popular search engine, offers excellent help screens for its advanced search options.

Google

http://www.google.com

Google is the first search engine to consider. It is powerful and easy to use, with a crawler-based service, which means that the engine "crawls" the Internet looking for relevant Web sites. Google is everywhere; it has saturated the Web, integrating itself into every market. Indeed, anyone can add a Google search bar to a Web site.

For more information about how to optimize the Google search, click on "Advanced Search." Google has a unique feature, the "Feeling Lucky" button which takes you straight to the hit Google thinks is most likely to fit your search criteria. Google's "Groups" link allows you to search the archives of USENET discussion groups.

Google is currently developing more links to online books. If Google finds a book that seems relevant to your search, it will be listed along with other links on your search results page. Or, you can search for books directly by choosing the "Print" link which, at press time, was accessible through the "More" link on the Google main page.

WEB SEARCH ENGINES AND DIRECTORIES

Yahoo!, http://www.yahoo.com offers a keyword search engine, a search engine based on a subject director and free email.

Yahoo!
http://www.yahoo.com

Yahoo! is an excellent keyword search engine. What also makes Yahoo! special is a separate directory engine created and managed by humans that offers links organized by subjects such as "Arts and Humanities" and "Entertainment." At present, Yahoo! makes its directory a little hard to find. Instead of entering a term in the search box, click on the word "More" just above, and you will see a link to the directory. Or go directly to http://search.yahoo.com/dir. Click on a major heading in the directory, and you will reach a list of subtopics. You can also do a keyword search within a subject category. Serious content only is here; the jokers, misinformers, and adult sites hoping to attract your business by misdirecting you to their Web sites have been edited out. But there are limits to the number of Web sites that can be reviewed by humans. Therefore, Yahoo! uses other methods to provide wider keyword coverage of the Internet though their more visible search box.

YAHOO! SEARCH

Web | Images | Video | Local | **Directory** | more »

[Directory Search]

Features and Editors' Picks

Yahoo! Picks: 360cities - Explore 360-degree, panoramic views of Prague, Moscow, Vienna, Venice, Los Angeles, Belgrade, and Syria....

Browse Yahoo!'s categorized guide to the Web.

Arts & Humanities	Health	Social Science
Business & Economy	News & Media	Society & Culture
Computers & Internet	Recreation & Sports	
Education	Reference	Other:
Entertainment	Regional	New Additions
Government	Science	RSS Feeds

Copyright © 2007 Yahoo! All rights reserved. Privacy / Legal - Submit Your Site

Yahoo! offers a directory of human generated links at http://search.yahoo.com/dir

WEB SEARCH ENGINES AND DIRECTORIES 29

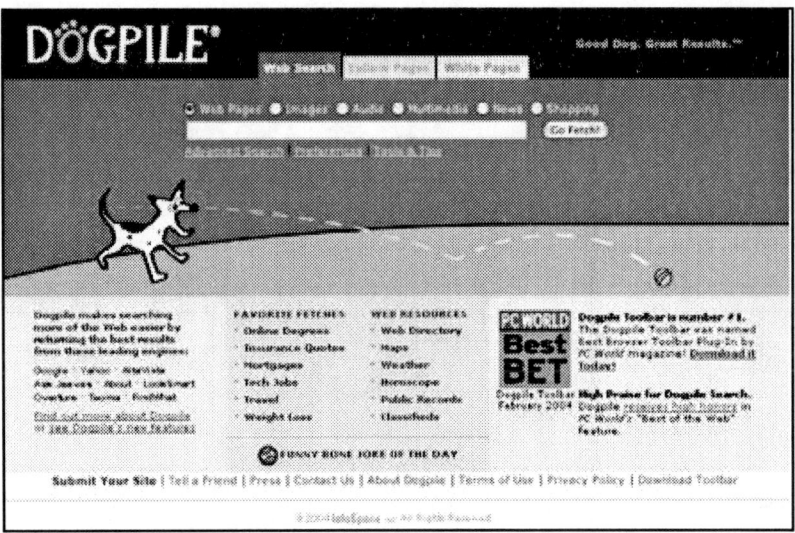

Dogpile is a metasearch engine which allows you to search several search engines at once.

Dogpile
http://www.dogpile.com

Despite the name—Dogpile is a serious search engine. Their goal is, though, to be better than Google, the current ruling monarch of search engines. How do they plan to distinguish themselves and change the face of Web research? They claim to be a newer, perhaps better, metasearch search engine. Metasearch search engines pull results from several different keyword search engines, allowing the user to search more of the Web for results. Dogpile.com merges results from Google, Yahoo!, AltaVista, Ask Jeeves, About, and LookSmart. Dogpile utilizes clustering technology, so results are given by category as well as in standard search format. It also clearly marks which links are commercially-sponsored, and users can request results by relevance or by search engine by simply clicking on a link.

Try the "Advanced Web Search" link which offers several types of searches, including the use of Boolean operators (AND, OR, NOT). See the box in this chapter labeled "Tools: Refining Your Search" for a discussion of Boolean operators and other advanced search features.

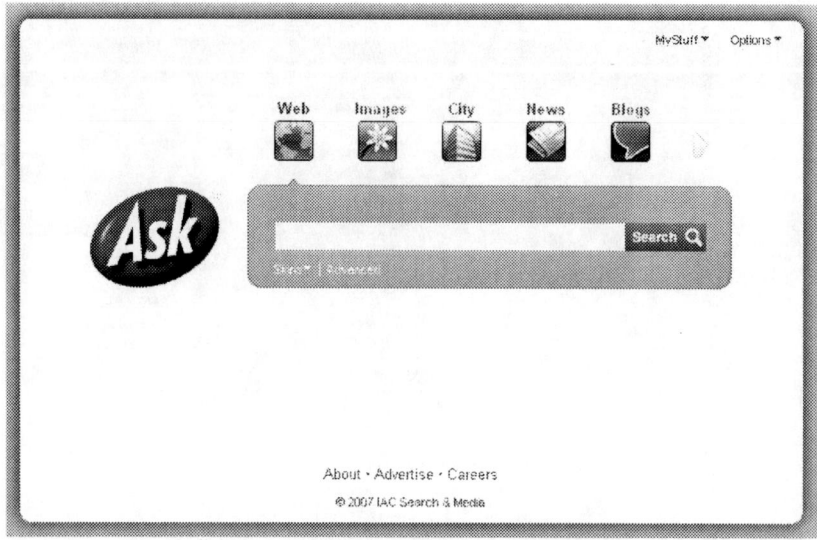

Enter search questions in plain language at Ask.

Ask
http://www.ask.com

This search engine allows you to enter a whole question rather than just key words. For example, you could ask questions such as "When is Mother's Day in 2005?" or "Who is Ray Bradbury?" Ask provides a researcher with a list of results to answer your question along with a "Related Searches" section providing results to searches similar to the question asked.

Other Search Engines to Try

AltaVista

http://www.altavista.com

AltaVista is a powerful engine for experienced users, allowing, for example, searching for an exact phrase, searching within the title of an HTML document, and searching for documents that link to a particular web address.

Ixquick

http://www.ixquick.com

Ixquick, like Dogpile, is a meta search engine, which means it searches many search engines at the same time. Ixquick's results are ranked based on other search engines' rankings and deletes duplicates from the results list.

AOL Search

http://aolsearch.aol.com from within AOL

http://search.aol.com outside AOL

AOL users may prefer to use their built-in search engine, AOL Search, because it also provides links to content available only within AOL. A crawler-based engine, it also gives Web links in a manner similar to Google's.

Tools: Refining Your Search

All search engines provide advanced search features that allow you to enter more information than key words and, thus, narrow the search to filter out irrelevant sites. Here are some tips that work in most engines:

- Click on Advanced Search or Help on the search engine's main page. You will receive a dialog page that allows you to limit your search in a variety of ways including additional key words, language, and file format. For example, if you are looking for images, you can specify .gif, .jpeg, or other image file formats.
- Quote marks: Use quote marks around your search to limit results to words in a specific order grouped together. This tool is useful for searching for phrases or multiple word concepts such as "To be or not to be" or "dietary supplement." Most search engines will recognize two capitalized words in a row as a search string, such as Ray Bradbury or Star Wars.
- The plus sign (+) tells a search engine that all results must contain the word it precedes. For example, +Bush +Runsfield would result in hits with both names.
- The minus sign (-) tells the search engine to ignore any results that contain a particular word. For example, Shakespeare –plays would return hits about other aspects of Shakespeare such as his poetry.
- Related searches: In most search engines, if you search for Shakespeare, you may be offered links to related searches such as Shakespeare's Sonnets, life of William Shakespeare, and the complete works of Shakespeare. These related search links generally appear near the top of a page of hits on a topic.
- Find Similar: Some search engines offer the option "find similar" following a hit of a link to similar pages.
- Search Within: Several of the major search engines, including Google, Lycos, and Yahoo! allow you to do a second search on the results of a first search. For example, if you search for "abortion" and receive too many hits, you can use the search within feature to search for a "third-term" within the hits you have already generated.
- Boolean operators—Use words such as AND, OR, and NOT to limit your search. For example, if you use the keywords radioactive waste, some of the search engines will return hits for either radioactive or waste. If you type radioactive AND waste, however, the search engine will look for those two terms together. If you use the keywords Shakespeare AND NOT plays you will receive hits about Shakespeare but not his plays. Not all search engines recognize Boolean operators, however. You can find out which search engines support which terms at Search Engine Watch, http://www.searchenginewatch.com.

Librarian-Reviewed Directories and Search Engines

One of the best ways for students to find Internet resources is through several indexing projects sponsored by major libraries. In the case of each directory/search tool, librarians have personally reviewed and selected Web sites that are of value to academic researchers, including both students and faculty. These indexing Web sites may be organized by subject area, in addition to having keyword search engines. You might find it useful to bypass traditional search engines such as Google and Excite and to begin research for a term paper with these subject directories or engines. Thus, you might quickly locate the most authoritative Web sites without having to wade through masses of sites looking for the reliable ones. All of these engines/directories are organized somewhat differently, so you might want to browse through them and select two or three that look user friendly to you.

Bub Link
http://bubl.ac.uk/link

BUBL features a subject directory, in addition to a search engine, and offers a minimum of five selected resources for every subject indexed. It catalogs over 11,000 resources, carefully chosen in all academic disciplines, which increases each included site's credibility. The subject terms used are loosely based on the LCSH (Library of Congress Subject Headings) but have been adapted and expanded to make the subject index and search engine easier to use.

Hot Paper Topics
http://library.sau.edu/bestinfo/Hot/hotindex.htm

This site features librarian-researched links to credible sites for typical term paper topics such as attack on America/terrorism, bioethical issues, censorship, drug issues, Enron, gender issues, gun control, health care reform, human rights, and identity theft. See also the links on the "Best Info on the Net" Web site, http://library.sau.edu/bestinfo/Librarians/intergen.htm.

Infomine
http://infomine.ucr.edu

Infomine is a librarian-built subject index and search engine designed for faculty, students, and researchers. It is divided into major collections: biological, agricultural, and medical sciences; business and economics; cultural diversity and ethnic resources; electronic journals; government documents; K-12 instructional resources; university instructional resources; internet enabling tools; maps and GIS; physical sciences, engineering, computer science, and math; social sciences and humanities; and visual and performing arts.

Internet Public Library
http://www.ipl.org

The Reference Center at the Internet Public Library divides Web resources into sections for arts and humanities, business, computers, education, entertainment, health, government, regional, science and technology, and social science. The "Ask a Question" section allows the user to send a query, and a real librarian will respond to questions generally in a few days. Connect to the "Ask a Question" Web page for instructions on submitting a question. The "Reading Room" provides access to standard reference texts such as almanacs, calendars, and dictionaries, as well as links to other Internet finding tools.

Internet Scout Project
http://scout.wisc.edu

The Internet Scout Project is not exactly a library project, but numerous librarians and educators are involved in its indexing. Sponsored by the National Science Foundation, the Internet Scout Project offers timely information to the education community about valuable Internet resources. Among its services is the searchable weekly Scout Report which features Web site reviews.

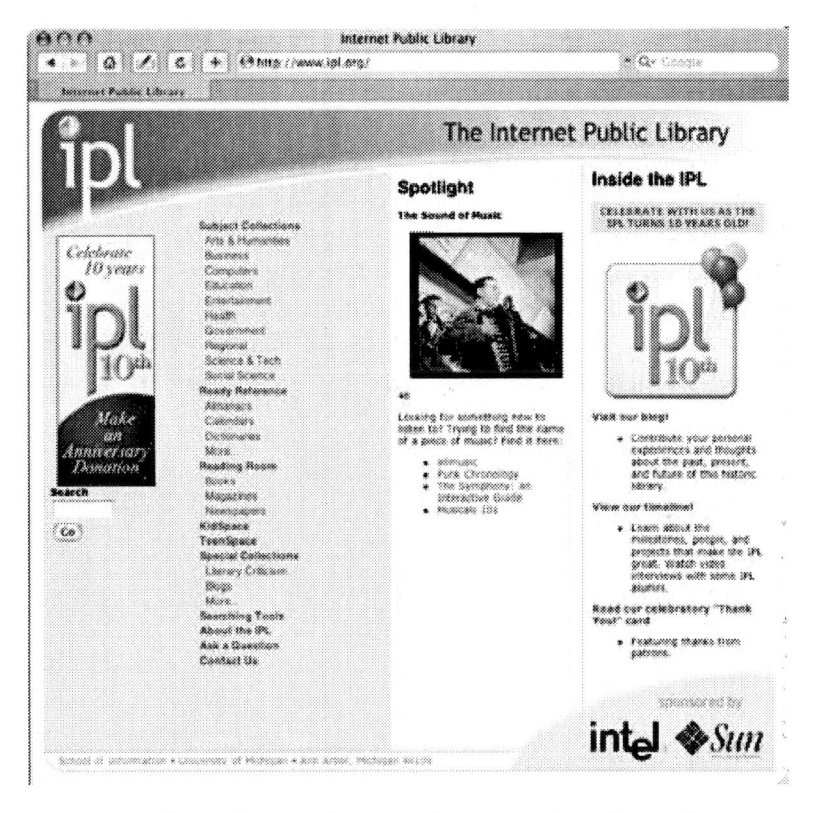

Internet Public Library offers a subject directory for Web resources, access to reference texts and periodicals, and an "Ask a Question" feature that sends information queries to librarians.

Librarians' Index to the Internet
http://lii.org

The Librarians' Index to the Internet prides itself for providing "Information You Can Trust." It is a searchable, annotated subject directory of more than 12,000 Internet resources selected by librarians for their value to students, librarians, and other researchers. Every site linked is reviewed at least twice before added to the Index, and the current inventory of links is reviewed constantly to eliminate dead links.

WWW Virtual Library
http://vlib.org

The WWW Virtual Library is the oldest human-screened index of Web sites. It was begun by CERN, the center for high-energy physics research where the Web was begun. Today, the WWW Virtual Library is organized and maintained by a group of volunteers. Organizations or individuals who have an extensive collection of links on a particular topic offer them to the library, and, if selected, a link is added to that collection. The library is quite extensive, and not all pages are located at CERN. The WWW Virtual Library does now also offer a keyword search option, in addition to the index.

Government Documents

More and more government institutions and agencies now publish many of their documents on the World Wide Web. It certainly saves taxpayer dollars to do so, and it also makes documents more accessible to the general public. Try one or more of the gateway sites mentioned below.

FirstGov
http://www.usa.gov

The federal government provides FirstGov as an easy access point or "front door" which links to more 186 million Web pages from federal and state governments, most of which are not available through commercial Web sites. You can find, for example, everything from books in the Library of Congress to real-time tracking of a NASA space mission. FirstGov even offers a special Web page that collects information for students about financial aid and careers.

FirstGov is the federal government's gateway to Web-based information from federal and state agencies and institutions.

Thomas Legislative Information
http://thomas.loc.gov

This link provides information about pending legislation and other matters relevant to the United States Congress. It offers a full text of the Congressional Record, public laws since 1973, committee reports, and much more.

Federal Information Center
http://fic.info.gov

The Federal Citizen Information Center (FCIC) supplies answers to questions about consumer problems and government services. For example, if you want to know more about social security benefits, you can find a jargon-free explanation at this site. Also, it offers "before you buy" information about consumer products, as well as a list of the best places to send a consumer complaint.

The Federal Web Locator
http://www.lib.auburn.edu/madd/docs/fedloc.html

The Center for Information Law and Policy offers this gateway to federal agencies and institutions, in addition to non-government federally-related sites.

Core Documents of the U.S. Democracy
http://www.gpoaccess.gov/coredocs.html

The Government Printing Office (GPO) maintains a digital collection of the basic federal government documents that "define our democratic society." The collection includes the Constitution, the Bill of Rights, landmark Supreme Court decisions, the Budget, the Census Catalog, and the US Government Manual.

CHAPTER 4:

The Invisible Web

The "visible web" is the part of the Web you can access from a search engine such as Google or a subject directory such as the one in Yahoo. The "invisible web" is the content available through the Web that you cannot access directly from a search engine or subject directory. This includes information from databases focused on specialized topics, as well as articles from newspapers, magazines, and journals. Database information is not stored in typical Web pages but is generated for each search query and may also require registration or entrance through a gateway search page. You cannot locate the information from periodicals in a more conventional search because search engines do not penetrate into the subpages of periodicals. Indeed, most publications require registration and a password (often for free) in order to obtain access to articles. Despite its "hidden" nature, the information from the invisible Web may be some of the most useful you can find.

Online Databases

Thousands of specialized databases that offer statistics and other information on a wide variety of topics are available through the Web. But how do you find them? One way is through a search engine such as Google, using the word "database" as one of your

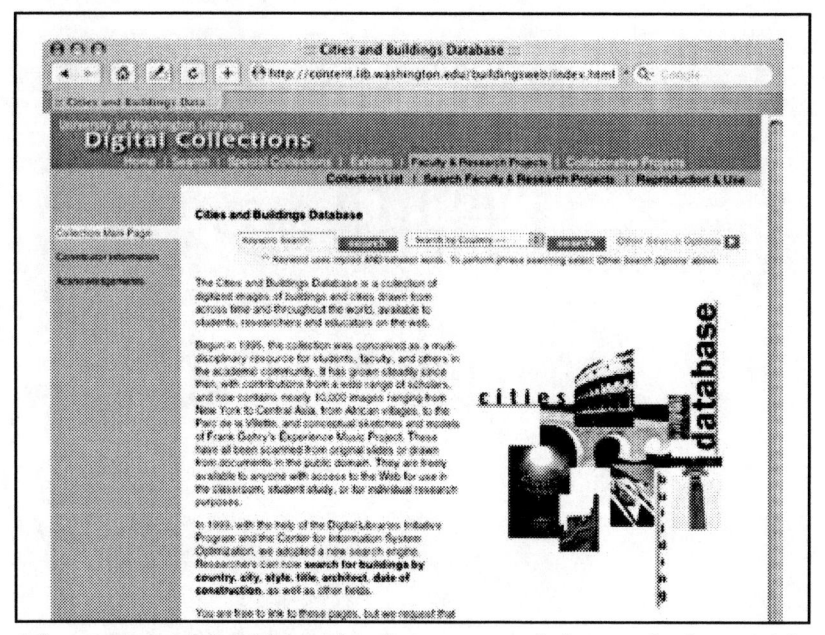

The Cities and Buildings database is one of thousands that can be found in the "invisible Web."

key word search terms. For example, if you search for "AIDS database" in Google, http://www.google.com, you will receive links to such sites as AEGIS, one of the largest HIV/AIDS databases in the world; the Africa HIV/AIDS Research Database, which tracks the spread of the disease in Africa; and the HIV/AIDS Surveillance Data Base maintained by the U.S. Bureau of the Census. The UC Berkeley Library offers an online tutorial to the invisible web at this address: http://www.lib.berkeley.edu/TeachingLib/Guides/Internet/InvisibleWeb.html#How. Also, Wikipedia has an up-to-date article about invisible web resources, http://en.wikipedia.org/wiki/invisible_web.

Magazines and Newspapers

Although not generally labeled as part of the invisible Web, online periodicals qualify because, like databases, you generally cannot access their articles directly from a search engine or directory. The *New York Times, Time, Newsweek,* and many other print publications offer full-text articles in special online editions of their print publications. To access the content of these or other periodicals on the Web, you must link to the main page of the publication to do a search.

Like other resources on the Web, several paths exist to reach publications, including searching by publication title in a search engine. There are also sites which index magazines, newspapers, and journals.

Using the publication's search feature, you can often access recent articles for free. The publication may charge a small fee for articles in the archives, however. You can, though, locate an article in a publication's archive and copy the article's title, author, date, and page. For a free copy of the article, you can then locate it in one of your library's subscription databases (see Chapter 2) or the library's periodical or microfilm sections.

Examples of Popular Newspapers and Magazines

New York Times
http://www.nytimes.com

Time
http://www.time.com

THE INVISIBLE WEB   43

U.S. News
http://www.usnews.com

Newsweek
http://www.msnbc.msn.com, select link to *Newsweek*

Web Links to Newspapers and Magazines

If you know the name of the publication you want, you can search for the name in any search engine. If you are looking for magazines on a particular topic or newspapers in a certain region or country, you can use the following Web sites which index newspapers and magazines.

Newsdirectory
http://www.newsdirectory.com

Yahoo!'s magazine list
http://dir.yahoo.com/News_and_Media/Magazines

Yahoo!'s newspaper list
http://dir.yahoo.com/News_and_Media/Newspapers

Internet Public Library (worldwide publications)
http://www.ipl.org/div/news

Newspapers.com (by country and by subject)
http://www.newspapers.com

CHAPTER 5:
Documentation

Avoid Plagiarism

Plagiarism is defined by the Writing Program Administrators (WPA), a group of English professors who direct college composition programs: "In an instructional setting, plagiarism occurs when a writer deliberately uses someone else's language, ideas, or other original (not common-knowledge) material without acknowledging its source." A keyword here is "deliberately." Instructors, however, may have difficulty distinguishing between accidental and deliberate plagiarism. The burden is upon you as the writer to give credit where credit is due. These are some examples of plagiarism:

- Turning in a paper that was written by someone else as your own. This includes obtaining a paper from an Internet term paper mill.
- Copying a paper or any part of a paper from a source without acknowledging the source in the proper format.
- Paraphrasing materials from a source without documentation.
- Copying materials from a text but treating it as your own, leaving out quotation marks and acknowledgement.

Choosing When to Give Credit

Need to Document	No Need to Document
• When you are using or referring to somebody else's words or ideas from a magazine, book, newspaper, song, TV program, movie, Web page, computer program, letter, advertisement, or any other medium. • When you use information gained through interviewing another person. • When you copy the exact words or a "**unique phrase**" from somewhere. • When you reprint any diagrams, illustrations, charts, and pictures. • When you use ideas that others have given you in conversation or over email.	• When you are writing your own experiences, your own observations, your own insights, your own thoughts, your own conclusions about a subject. • When you are using "**common knowledge**" — folklore, common sense observations, shared information within your field of study or cultural group. • When you are compiling generally accepted facts. • When you are writing up your own experimental results.

The Online Writing Lab (OWL) at Purdue University provides an excellent handout on avoiding plagiarism, including this box about when to give credit to sources. See http://owl.english.purdue.edu.

When is it necessary to cite a source? If you are writing that the Space Shuttle Columbia disaster happened in 2003, do you need to cite your source? No, because you could find that information in any of a number of places. What if you use information from a *New York Times* article about how U.S. fast food eating habits are spreading to Europe? Yes, if you are going to paraphrase or quote from the article. The table above, from the Purdue University Online Writing Lab, gives more examples of when to cite sources.

Documenting Sources

Academic writing mandates students document their sources. Documenting sources allows the reader to evaluate the writer's research in regard to value and credibility. Several styles of documentation are widely acceptable in the university, to include MLA (Modern Language Association), APA (American Psychological

Association), CBE (Council of Biology Editors), also called Scientific Style, and CMS (Chicago Manual of Style). This book focuses on MLA and APA styles. Each style of documentation offers both parenthetical (in-text) documentation and bibliographical documentation. In other words, every source must be cited within the text and at the end of the work. Recent technological advances have opened a wealth of electronic databases and independent Web sites offering instant access to valuable sources.

Students should not feel it is necessary to memorize documentation citation formats. They can always refer to the official handbooks for MLA, APA, CBE, and Chicago documentation styles. The Purdue University Online Writing Lab (OWL) offers an excellent summary of the different documentation styles and links to resources for each. See http://owl.english.purdue.edu/handouts/research/r_docsources.html. You can also go to the home page, http://owl.english.purdue.edu and select "Handouts and Materials," then "Research and Documenting Sources," that will lead you to an abundance of useful handouts. Practice in proper documentation will ensure a better understanding of academic writing, familiarity with sources, and the ethical responsibility of crediting original authors.

Challenges in Documenting Electronic Publications

Finding the Persistent Link

When retrieving an item from an electronic database or Web site, it is essential to document the correct URL (Universal Resource Locator), so that ideally a reader can find that particular item by simply going to the documented URL address (persistent link). In the case of a Web site, students are often challenged in deciding which address to cite since Web sites offer many pages within that particular Web site. In regard to citing from a text on a Web site, students should refer to the address at the top of their screen and cite the entire URL address for that particular page. This is usually a very long address. The persistent link may be more difficult to find for electronic databases such as Academic Search Premier or Lexis-Nexis. Most texts from databases cite an address on the bottom of the item's page, but this is not the persistent link because a reader cannot type in this address and link directly to the text. Rather, the reader must go through the "front door" or designated home page for the database. Therefore, the reader's retrieval of that particular text is only possible by the reader connecting to the database and doing a search for the text.

Finding Page Numbers

When retrieving an item from an electronic database or Web site, students are often given a choice of opening either an HTML (Web page) document or a PDF (Adobe Portable Document Format) document. A problem exists since students are required to cite the actual page numbers of an item and only the PDF format show these page numbers. Since many articles are not offered in the PDF format, students cannot cite the actual page numbers.

MLA Style

For MLA style, also refer to the *MLA Handbook for Writers of Research Papers* and the MLA Web site, http://www.mla.org.

Bibliographical Documentation

In MLA Style, this is called either the Works Cited page or an Annotated Bibliography. The title, Works Cited or Annotated Bibliography, should appear centered on the top margin of the last page of a researched essay. The Works Cited page should be double-spaced with no extra line spacing between entries. The first line of each entry begins at the margin, and all subsequent lines of a particular entry are indented 5 spaces on the left margin. All entries should be in alphabetical order. The Annotated Bibliography is formatted like the Works Cited page with the addition of an annotation or description of the source in a paragraph following the citation. The following entries are typical citations for an MLA style. Examples are offered for both print, online, and database versions, when applicable.

Book or Novel
Nicolson, Adam. *Seize the Fire: Heroism, Duty, and the Battle of Trafalgar*. New York: HarperCollins, 2005.

Book with Multiple Editors
Mennuti, Rosemary B., Arthur Freeman, and Ray W. Christner, eds. *Cognitive-behavioral Interventions: A Handbook for Practice.* New York: Routledge, 2006.

Online Editon of Book or Novel
James, Henry. *The American.* 1877. 15 Apr. 2005. <http://eserver.org/fiction/novel.html>.

Scholarly Article
Andrews, Howard. "Writing and the Internet." *Teaching English in the Two Year College* 21 (1999): 233-51.

Scholarly Article Online
Kimihiko, Yoshii and Tonogai Yasuhide. "Water Content Using Karl-Fisher Aquametry and Loss on Drying Determinations Using Thermogravimeter for Pesticide Standard Materials." *Journal of Health Science* 50.2 (2004): 142-47. 2 Jun. 2005. <http://www.jstage.jst.go.jp/browse/jhs/50/2/_contents>.

(Notice that this entry is for an article in a journal with text available online. The print information, such as the volume number, is given first. Then the link to the online text is given in brackets.)

Scholarly Article from Online Database Available through a Library
McMichael, Anthony. J. "Population, Environment, Disease, and Survival: Past Patterns, Uncertain Futures." 145-48. Academic Universe: Medical. Lexis-Nexis. California Digital Lib. 22 May 2002 <http://web.lexis-nexis.com>.

(Notice that the Web page cited above is the home page for the database.)

Article from a Magazine
Deboer, Peter. "Junior Achievers." *Sports Illustrated* 6 Jun. 2005: 17-18.

Article from a Magazine Online
Banks, Suzy. "Hill Country." *Texas Monthly Online.* Apr. 2005. 15 Apr. 2005 <http://www.texasmonthly.com/previous/2005-04-01/feature3>.

Magazine Article from an Online Database Available through a Library
Seltzer, Larry. "Tales of a Professional Social Engineer." *PC Magazine* 7 Jun. 2005: 105-111. Academic Search Premier. University of Texas at El Paso Digital Lib. 22 Apr. 2005 <http://www.ebscohost.com>.
(Notice that the Web page cited above is the home page for the database.)

Newspaper Article
Trembacki, Paul. "Brees Hopes to Win Heisman for Team." *The Dallas Morning News* 5 Dec. 2000: 20.

Newspaper Article Online
Pear, Robert. "States Intervene After Drug Plans Hit Early Snags." *New York Times* 7 Jan. 2006. 15 Feb. 2006 <http://www.nytimes.com>.

Newspaper Article from Online Database Available through a Library
Kolata, Gina. "Koreans Report Ease in Cloning for Stem Cells." *New York Times* 20 May 2005: A1. Academic Search Premier. University of Texas at El Paso Digital Lib. 5 Mar. 2005 <http://www.ebscohost.com>.

(Notice that the Web page cited above is the home page for the database.)

Government Document
"El Chamizal Dispute: Compliance with Convention of the Chamizal." 1964. *US Senate Hearing.* Cleofas Calleros Papers. University of Texas at El Paso Library Special Collections. 33-9.

Government Document Online
Travis, William Barret. "Letter from the Alamo, 1836." Texas State Library & Archives Commission. 15 Apr. 2005 <http//www.tslstate.tx.us/treasures/republic/Alamo/travis01.gov>.

Government Document from Online Database Available through a Library
"United Nations Resolutions on Operation Desert Storm." Aug-Nov 1990. *Essential Documents in American History: 1492-Present.* 1-17 Academic Search Premier. University of Texas at El Paso Digital Lib. <http://www.ebscohost.com>.

Educational Web Site (they usually end in edu)
Turner, Logan. "Texas Farming: Life of a Migratory Wheat Cutter." Interview with Jack Waldroop. Texas Farming Oral History Files. 2004. 15 Apr. 2005. <http://www.texasfarmingoralhistoryfiles.edu>.

MLA Parenthetical or (In-text) Documentation

Parenthetical documentation refers to the process of citing sources within the text. Citing sources within the text is necessary for students to indicate when they are using the words, thoughts, or ideas that are not their own and borrowed from an outside source. Whether students use a direct quote, a paraphrase or summary of the information, they must properly provide credit to the original author(s) of that source. Using appropriate sources for support and documenting these sources accurately adds to the credibility and value of a student's essay. The following examples provide a guideline to proper parenthetical documentation.

Direct Quote (three lines or less)

"Scientists estimate that the rangewide population of the San Joaquin kit fox prior to 1930 was 8,000…" (Conover 44).

Direct Quote (more than three lines) (Indent 10 spaces and block.)

Conover's 2001 study of the San Joaquin kit fox found the following:
          For the most part, in the "real" world, kit foxes escape their predators and the high temperatures of their desert environment by spending the day underground in a den. In Bakersfield, they follow suite. Kit foxes move every couple of weeks to a new den. Moving to different dens may be one reason why they have persisted; the constantly changing abodes provided new places to hide. (199)

Direct Quote when the author is named in the text:

Hildebrand states that, "generals of Alexander the Great brought news to Europe of vegetable wool which grew in tufts of trees in India" (144).

Information from printed source, but it is not a direct quote:

It is common to see an Osprey make its nest on an electric power pole (Askew 34).

Electronic Sources Many electronic sources are not numbered with pages unless it is a PDF file. If paragraphs are numbered, use numbers following the abbreviation, par. Most often the source will not have page, paragraph, section or screen numbers. In this case, include no numbers in the parenthesis.

(Bussell par. 3)

APA Style

For APA style, also refer to the *Publication Manual of the American Psychological Association* and the Web site provided by the American Psychological Association which has a FAQ about documenting sources, http://www.apastyle.org.

Bibliographical Documentation

In APA Style, this is called either the References Page or Annotated Bibliography. The title, References or Annotated Bibliography, should appear centered on the top margin of the last page of a researched essay. The References or Annotated Bibliography page should be double-spaced with no extra line spacing between entries. The first line of each entry begins at the margin, and all subsequent lines of a particular entry are indented on the left margin 5 spaces for a References Page and 7 for an Annotated Bibliography. All entries should be in alphabetical order. The Annotated Bibliography is formatted like the References page with the addition of an annotation or description of the source in a paragraph following the citation. The following entries are typical citations for APA style. Examples are offered for both print, online, and database versions, when applicable.

Book or Novel
Nicolson, A. (2005). *Seize the fire: Heroism, duty, and the battle of Trafalgar.* New York: HarperCollins.

Book or Novel with Multiple Editors
Mennuti, R.B., Freeman, A., and Christner, R.W. (Eds.). (2006). *Cognitive-behavioral interventions in educational settings: A handbook for practice.* New York: Routledge.

Book or Novel Online Edition
James, H.(1960). *The American.* Retrieved April 15, 2005, from http://eserver.org/fiction/novel.html

Scholarly Article
Andrews, H. (1992). Writing and the Internet. *Teaching English in the Two-Year College, 21*, 233-251.

Scholarly Article Online
Kimihiko, Y., & Yasuhide, T. (2004). Water content using Karl-Fisher aquametry and loss on drying determinations using thermogravimeter for pesticide standard materials. *Journal of Health Science , 50*, 142-147. Retrieved June 2, 2005, from http://www.jstage.jst.go.jp/browse/jhs/50/2/_contents

Scholarly Article from Online Database Available through a Library
McMichael, A. J. (2002). Population, environment, disease, and survival: Past patterns, uncertain futures. *Lancet, 30* 1145-1148. Retrieved May 22, 2002, from Academic Universe: Medical. Lexis-Nexis.

Article from a Magazine
Deboer, P. (2005, June). Junior achievers. *Sports Illustrated,* pp. 17-18.

Article from a Magazine Online
Banks, S. (2005, April). Hill country. *Texas Monthly Online*. Retrieved April 15, 2005, from http://www.texasmonthly.com/previous/2005-04-01/feature3

Magazine Article from an Online Database Available through a Library
Seltzer, L. (2005, June). Tales of a professional social engineer. *PC Magazine*, pp. 105-111. Retrieved April 22, 2005, from Academic Search Premier.

Newspaper Article
Trembacki, P.(2000, December 5). Brees hopes to win Heisman for team. *The Dallas Morning News*, p. 20.

Newspaper Article Online
Aguilar, M.(2005, March 28). Miners anxious to get back to work. *The El Paso Times*. Retrieved April 2005, from http:www.elpasotimesonline/03/28/05.htm

Newspaper Article from Online Database Available through a Library
Kolata, G. (2005, May 20). Koreans report ease in cloning for stem cells. *New York Times*, p. A1. Retrieved March 5, 2005, from Academic Search Premier.

Government Document
El chamizal dispute: Compliance with convention of the chamizal. (1964*). US Senate Hearing.* Cleofas Calleros Papers. University of Texas at El Paso Library Special Collections (#33-9).

Government Document Online
Travis, W. B. (2005). Letter from the Alamo, 1836. Retrieved April 15, 2005, from *Texas State Library & Archives Commission,* http//www.tslstate.tx.us/treasures/republic/Alamo/travis01.gov

Government Document from Online Database Available through a Library
United Nations resolutions on Operation Desert Storm.(1990*) Essential Documents in American History: 1492-Present.* Retrieved June 1, 2005, from Academic Search Premier.

Educational Web Site (they usually end in edu)
Turner, L. (2004). Texas farming: Life of a migratory wheat cutter. Interview with Jack Waldroop. *Texas Farming Oral History Files*. Retrieved April 15, 2005, from http://www.texasfarmingoralhistoryfiles.edu

APA Parenthetical or (In-text) Documentation

Direct Quote (three lines or less)

"Scientists estimate that the rangewide population of the San Joaquin kit fox prior to 1930 was 8,000..." (Conover, 2001, p. 44).

Direct Quote (more than three lines) (Indent 5 spaces and block.)

Conover's 2001 study of the San Joaquin kit fox found the following:

> For the most part, in the "real" world kit foxes escape their predators and the high temperatures of their desert environment by spending the day underground in a den. In Bakersfield, they follow suit. Kit foxes move every couple of weeks to a new den. Moving to different dens may be one reason why they have persisted; the constantly changing abodes provided new places to hide. (p. 199)

Direct Quote when the author is named in the text:

Hildebrand (2004) stated that, "generals of Alexander the Great brought news to Europe of vegetable wool which grew in tufts of trees in India" (p. 144).

Information from printed source, but it is not a direct quote:

It is common to see an Osprey make its nest on an electric power pole (Askew, year, p. 34).

Naming the author of a reference in your text, but not using a direct quote:

Thompson (2002) maintained that…

In 2002, Thompson discovered…

Electronic Sources (Again, many electronic sources are not numbered with pages. If your source provides section notations or paragraph number, indicate those. Use the paragraph ¶ symbol or the abbreviation para. and number.)

(Bussell, 2000, ¶ 9)

(Morrison, 2001, Introductory section, para. 2)